Eternal Embers

Chloe Cullen

Presentation by *BookLeaf Publishing*

Web: www.bookleafpub.com

E-mail: info@bookleafpub.com

ISBN : 9789357445467

First edition 2021

DEDICATION

Mum, Dad, Laura, Pepper and Jake, you are the best forever and always.

ACKNOWLEDGEMENT

Thank you to my Mum and Dad, my sister Laura and my cats Pepper and Jake for encouraging and believing in me even when I do not believe in myself.

Thank you to anyone who picks up this book and reads even just one word. Putting words to paper and connecting with others through the ink on the pages means more to me than money, fame or glory. This is my first book and I am by no means an expert but this has taught me that when something makes you happy, jump for it and do not stop because of the fear of not being enough, whether that is the fear of not being good enough or smart enough. All you really need is passion and nothing else matters.

Hope and Misery

Faceless and faithless, lost and alone
Hard to be found in a world full of frowns
The grey falls and the haze stays
The hope diminishes, the will to go on fades

I don't want the world to see me
All I can do is run and hide
In this world where nothing and nobody is safe
My body is left in a state of crave

Crave of a feeling, crave of a touch
That makes this planet feel less lonely, less hurt
and less still
The more I want it, the more they laugh
Taunting and haunting my mind
Nothingness is loud and noise is quiet
Hope is misery and sadness makes me feel alive

Was It Love?

If love is in the way your lips touch mine
Then why can't I taste it?
If love is in your familiar safe scent
Then why can't I smell it?
If love is in the sparkle of your eyes
Then why can't I see it?
If love is in the passion of your words
Then why can't I hear it?
If love is in the way you hold and graze my
supple skin
Then why can't I feel it?

If love is truly all of these things and more
Then why I am always left feeling so raw
Knowing you show these things but I can't taste
them, smell them, see them, hear them or feel
them,
It raises the question, were they truly ever there
at all?

Shattered

I used to hold my breath,
And hope that the next one would never come
I used to take a step,
And pray that the next would be my last

Every little thing felt like it was tumbling
It shattered me inside;
And ricochet in the light for all eyes

Someday

The moon casts a glow
The sun casts a shadow
The stars cast a spotlight
The planets fall in a row

Lines can be round
Circles can be straight
Choice can be a reason
A question can be fate

If you want it, reach for it
Even if it hurts along the way
If you have it, spread it
Even if others' think they don't need it

If you mean it, show it
Even if you think it's crystal clear
Because in the end, we are billions of atoms, all
looking for someone, something, somewhere
With hope and love and strength and care,
someday we will get there

Playing With Love

I doubt your words, and you doubt mine
I took your hand, and you let go in time

You asked me to stay, and I said no
I asked you to stay, and you did

You wanted ice cream, and I yearned for
cheesecake,
You favoured the beach, and I preferred the lake

I chose the inside, and you chose the out,
We slowly let this deepen our doubt

The pages keep turning, but we never meet on
the same one.
You are playing love, I am playing love, and we
are playing with love

Serenity

One breath, two breaths, three
Nose twitches and eyes open to see
Ears perk up and whiskers flare
Paws grip tightly to the arm of the chair

Tail flaps and eyes squint
Belly rises in a numerical sprint

Peace overcomes and eyes slowly close
The tail continues flapping and the dreams
finally arose

Finding That Something

Drowning in the quiet
I ask myself 'am I okay?
But the answer always equals minus

Staring at the blank wall, and looking for a sign
Memorising every detail, trying to find the
straight line

But nothing is that simple, it is never black and
white
There is no right and there is no wrong
The fear around my body just feels so tight

Will I ever find my true self
Will I ever know which road to take
I truly hope that one day, this life I can finally
make

Fine

It's fine
What do you mean it's fine?
What is fine?

I have nothing and no one
Not a single item to my name
I don't have you, and I don't have them
All I have is myself to blame

I tried so hard
And I failed so miserably
Was it all in vain
When in the end fine is nonexistent to me

My Light Source

Even in the darkest of days
You are the source of light
Even in the deepest of depths
You help me fight to the surface

The days drag on, and I push you away
But you still stayed by my side
The fights enrage, and the hurtful words pierce
And the hope inside me died

I can't expect you to stay and tell me it will be
okay
I can't expect you to say it's fine, and those
words didn't mean a thing
Because the guilt courses through me, and the
resentment will build in you
As this pattern increases, hurt you more I do

Five years later and my light has gone
No direct source from you for so long
But fall I didn't and die I did not
Because your memory and the lessons you
taught me were eventually enough to make the
hurt stop

I hope you are living now
And I hope you are happy
For whilst you may not realise this
You made me open my eyes and truly see what
life is all about

Finally Enough

You are there, but it is not enough
You look my way and smile
We walk towards each other, and you pass me by
No lingering look to share
Maybe that is all there is
Perhaps that is all there will ever be
A smile and the crossing of paths between you
and me

You talk to me, and it is almost enough
Passing words of little significance
But maybe more
All I can really be sure
Is that you walk straight back out the door

You see me, and it is enough
You look, I look
You touch, I touch
And the unspoken reassurance is spoken
I will be here from night to day and from day to
night
From summer to winter, to spring to autumn,
From life to death and from unknowing to can't
live without you

I am here

Is There Anything Out There?

I don't know where I am going
I don't know where I am
I twist and turn in all directions, but there is no
clear path ahead
I am grabbing onto an invisible rope in hopes I
will find my place
But this world has other plans for me
I have no saving grace

Grappling with the wind and fighting through
the thunder
The realisation that this is futile threatens to drag
me under
Despite the heavy droplets of rain and the grey
stormy sky
I look up above, and all I can wonder is why

Why am I me, and why are you, you?
Why am I standing here still while you are
effortlessly gliding through?
I try so hard still I get nowhere
Whilst you don't try, and you arrive somewhere

Is this all there is out there for me
Is this all that I can pursue
The empty nothing all around me
Just forever hoping for something true

The World As We Know It

In the blink of an eye, it fell
No life to live and no more dreams to sell
The end of the beginning and the beginning of
the end
It feels like it is something we will never
actually mend

All of it is so inconsequential, yet the crisis is
existential
War is ongoing, but some of them are old
Time heals all wounds, but that is just what I am
told

I do sit and wonder did we ever honestly have it
all
For our world was already a mess before the fall
We failed to see the beauty before less and less
Now it feels like it is all gone, and we are under
a constant state of duress

Ruled by these creatures who have no rules of
their own
It is more than unfortunate our children will
never experience what it is to be grown

Maybe that is a bad thing, yet maybe it is a
blessing in a world gone mad
All I know is that I miss certain things so bad

The smell of freshly cut grass and the feeling of
the breeze against my porcelain skin
Now all we have is darkness and damp
Stuck in this basement, one of many, without the
light of a lamp
This might be all we know and all we ever have
As long as you're by my side the hope for the
future is much more than a half

Waking Up

The Fourth of July fireworks exploding and
sailing high
The memory of you forever remains in the sky
Flying in that metal and defying all the odds
You were not made of steel, but you bravely did
your job

I hoped and prayed for your return until one day
you appeared
My heart no longer had to yearn
We spent days together living, being, seeing
Until finally you got on one knee and produced a
golden band

The years felt endless, and there was never any
despair
We laughed and loved and humourlessly cried
when you fell off that dining room chair
Evenings by the piano sipping bubbling liquid
It was honestly a splendid life we lived

Now I sharply awake in bed, and you are not
there

No remnants or clues of your being leads me to
despair
Panic overcomes as I pace back and forth
Racking my brain for memories and thinking
you could have gone up north

That is when I see the newspaper and read the
date and year
It is that time again when the Fourth of July
festivities are clear
My stomach drops, and sweat beads down my
forehead
I look at the date and realise I never actually left
my bed

It is still nineteen eighty-seven and the seventh
month of the year
I never thought those words would elicit a tear
My glass of water and gold earring lay on my
bedside chair alongside the image of us playing
with cars and planes in our hidden treehouse we
called our lair

That is when I remember the year before
You left to join a cause and go and fight a war
On the day of departure, you placed a kiss on my
head, and I still remember the last words you
said

"I will see you soon my love, we have forever",
but neither of us knew it would be the last words
I had from you to replay over and over in my
head

Now every morning, just like this one, I open
my eyes
I expect to see you lying by my side, but then I
remember, and the light in me dies
"I will never love again" are the words from my
tongue spoken, but you tell me you are already
gone, and from my restless sleep I am woken

One Day

One day you're here
One day you're there
One day I speak the truth
One day I dare

We have come a long way
Could we leave the past behind
Or will we stay stuck, still, fixated on those
memories that will only leave us blind

Blind in angst and blind in guilt
Blind in hope, enough to make our axis tilt
The world can be cruel, but your words were
worse
Piercing my atrium and entangling me in your
curse

What you've done to me, you've cast upon
many others
You said I was different, but you left me just as
easy like we were never once lovers
Did you mean anything you said
Or were they only empty, meaningless words
from something you once read

I needed you, and you were there
You pulled me out of my despair
Away from the pain, and away from the hurt
And into your arms where I thought I was safe,
but now all I feel is at the mercy of your strafe

Reminisce

We look back, and we reminisce
On all the memories and moments we so dearly
miss
Photos and videos may be something we
possess, but the films inside our minds are much
more valuable, and how we regress

Moments that make us laugh so hard and cry so
much
Life flashing before your eyes the love can only
be defined as a crutch
A crutch to help you keep on fighting and a
crutch to help make you see
That when we continue living, we carry our
loved ones with us much further beyond what
the blind eye can see, far beyond the waters of
the sea

Mind Gone

We knew each other from the hallways, passed
by each other many times
I guess it was so many that eventually, I learnt to
miss the signs
The things you said and what you did
The whole town warned me never to lift that lid

We both came from trouble, albeit different
types
We had a fair few run-ins where we both made
anger fuelled swipes
I am not sure where they came from or why we
played a game
Deep down I think it might be because we didn't
want the other to think we were lame

As we had more reasons to be in the same place
I started to become more energised at knowing I
would be met with the sight of your face
Looking at you differently I heard the unspoken
behind the words
It made me want to come back for seconds and
thirds

They say I have lost my mind to start having
these thoughts about you but I don't think I have
ever felt passion so true
Fuelled from an empty dislike encouraged by
others
I knew what I would choose if I had my druthers

You saw something in me that others didn't
Not even I knew about myself, and that made
life worth vivant
You said you saw me soar, and that it was more
beautiful than any feathered being you had ever
witnessed, but that you were dead weight which
was bad news for someone like me

You weren't supposed to care, and neither was I,
but now these breathless moments we share are
so much more than what started as a lie
Lying to ourselves and lying to others to keep
them happy was worth nothing when I saw you
so unhappy
If you are dead weight then I will give you a
wing so we can fly together and our hearts can
finally sing

Journey

That road trip I took was going to be a solitary
dull stint
Until I sat at a bar listening to you play, then
later you sat beside me and offered me a mint
Something so trivial yet means so much when I
looked you in the eyes and felt your touch

Your calloused hand brushed against my soft one
The oxymoron a mystery that made it all the
more fun
We conversed for hours until closing time crept
in
Then we said our goodbyes, and it felt like not
giving you my number was a sin

Sleep was restless, a tossing and turning type of
night
Faster than I appreciated it was daytime, and
through the curtains streamed the light
Getting out of the island of throws I had little
energy to put up a fight
I packed my case, showered and fresh, ready to
see the next sight

The car was old, but the message of this trip was
not something to be forgotten
I was doing this for her memory that I wanted to
wrap in cotton
Turning the corner from the entrance of the
motel my heart suddenly stopped
There was an empty space beside the concrete
curb where the engine, wheels, and metal were
once propped

Sat there in its place was a man on the curb
Guitar case beside him whilst he stared off into
the sunny city distance like he was reading a
riveting story blurb
He must have seen something I didn't
For all I witnessed was a town that was deficient

As if sensing my presence you turned around
and off wiped my frown
It was the same chestnut hair and blue eyes from
the night before
The same grin and energy that made my worries
fall

That is where the adventure began
In your wheels touring the places we both had
on our road trip itinerary plan

Making stops on the way to get to know each
other, ultimately trying to find reasons not to
stay
For you had your life, and I had mine
It was complicated, and we ran out of time

The dreaded day came when you had to leave
my side
I wanted to jump back in your car and share the
same ride
As much as the need was mighty the real-life
prevailed
We had to leave with the promise of seeing one
another again someday
Something I know we both hesitantly believed,
but vigorously craved

Fast forward one year, and the dust from life
transformations settled
Things develop, others evolve, and the
relationship I had was broken
It felt like a life change was the token
If I was being honest, the real reason my life was
at a standstill and had fallen apart was that the
boy I met in the bar and on the curb had stolen
my heart

Rushing to the bar where we first met

I watched on as another singer played
It felt reminiscent of how we first set our sights
on each other
The excitement bubbled inside when I saw him
slip in the chair beside me but when he pulled
his hat up to reveal his features the confusion on
my face was clear to see
Then came the tears and the torture as your
friend told me you had felt the same
You were on your way here when the flying
metal crashed, and you died in a mix of flames

My world fell apart that day, but at the same
time it was made
I knew the time we spent together had made me
unafraid
You taught me lessons on love and letting go,
and I taught you lessons on being open
We both helped fix each other after having been
broken

I am writing this to you, even though I know you
are dead, but I want you to know that no matter
what I will always keep your memory alive in
my head

No Choice

You pulled the trigger, but I held the smoking
gun
One of us surrendered, but still, none of us won
It isn't a game of right as much as it is wrong
The torture will continue for many years long

You left me with no choice
Nothing could stop you, not even a begging
decibel in my voice
There was nothing to salvage even though I tried
The evil inside you raged, and the good part of
you died

Many years later, that day still haunts me
My heart only keeps beating because of the hope
that you are now free
Free from the control and free from the torment
All I can hope is that wherever you are, you
know how much you meant

My Pack

We won this war, but the fight is not over
We need more luck than a four-leaf clover
That is not saying that we do not have the skill
But it was never in our nature to stand up and
kill

These are my people, and this is my team
We have each others' back, and we share the
same dream
We are only young but naive not still
For the things, we have seen sink into our brains
deeper than a drill

We are all different and unique in more than one
way
Each of us has an important part to play
We can only look forward and not look back
These are my friends, and this is my pack

Warmth and Wonder

White fluffy cotton falls at a steady rate
The blanket covered ground is losing visibility
as night arrives and it becomes late
The wooden log cabin is tucked snugly in the
forest
A warm cup of cocoa and marshmallows for she
was a ritualist

Carols are sung and gingerbread men are made
It would be a crime for the radio not to play
Slade
Family traditions and rites of passage are always
key
That magical feeling is a one hundred per cent
guarantee

Lights start to flicker, and soon we experience
the greatest technicolour
The trees come to life, and the tinsel
dramatically glitters leaving the world a lot less
duller
Happiness and the spirit of the time of the year
Anything is possible with some Christmas cheer

Stand Up

Once upon a time is a story often told
But do we learn the lesson, or does the telling
become old
We make the same mistakes over and over again
Can we ever learn from the past, or are we
burdened to ignore the pen?

The ink heeds a warning we shall not forget
Yet the world seems to recreate the same upset
Maybe in different forms and alternate
circumstance
In the end, it's all the same until we take a
different stance

It is time we stand up for change and fight for
the good
Listen carefully to the misunderstood
We need to come together with our fight aligned
For when we stand up for what is right, true
justice we will find